Published by
Western Psychological Services
12031 Wilshire Boulevard
Los Angeles, California 90025

International Standard Book Number: 0-87424-368-8

First printing .... March, 2000

1 2 3 4 5 6 7 8 9

christopher's Anger

by Denise Zuckerman, M.A.

illustrated by Jessica Sandek, B.F.A.

Published by

WPS®

Publishers   Distributors

Christopher gets angry.
He does not get angry like other people.

When Christopher's mother is angry, she yells.
She slams cupboard doors.
She screams for everyone to get out of the room.

When the yelling stops,
everything gets very quiet.
Mother says nothing for a while.

Christopher does not get angry that way.

When Christopher's father gets angry,
he moves really close to you and
shakes his finger in your face.

Sometimes he shakes *you*.
There are times when Father hits hard, really hard.
Then he hollers at the top of his lungs.
Sometimes the hollering is about something important.
Most of the time it is not.

Christopher does not get angry that way.

When Christopher's sister gets angry,
she becomes red in the face.
She pushes you, pinches you, gives you dirty looks,
digs her fingernails into your skin,
and hovers over you without saying a word.

Then she puts on her stereo headphones
and pretends that no one else exists.

Christopher does not get angry that way.

When Christopher's baby brother is angry,
he cries all the time.
He gags and chokes and screams and
makes all sorts of scary sounds.

Baby Brother falls asleep
when he is finally tired of screaming.

Christopher does not get angry that way.

When Christopher gets angry,
a black cloud appears above his head
and descends over him.

Giant balls of cotton fill his ears.

His stomach churns like a stormy sea.

A heavy scarf snakes around his neck.

A film of sticky plastic coats his skin.

Christopher tries to bang the cloud away.

He pulls at the cotton balls...

He expels the stormy sea...

He scratches at the scarf...

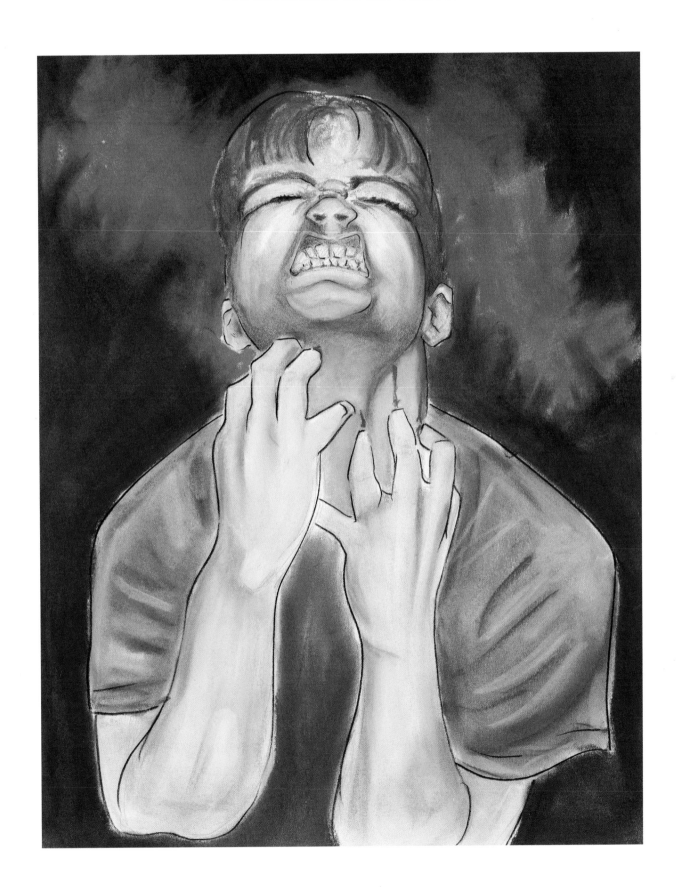

He bites at the plastic sticking to his body.

Mother, Father, Sister, and Baby Brother are bewildered when Christopher bangs his head, pulls his hair, vomits, scratches his neck, and bites his arms. They are frightened when he is angry. They do not understand. They do not get angry that way.

Mother and Father are concerned about Christopher.
They take him to a woman named Anna.
Anna is someone who helps people help themselves.
Adults and children go to her when they want to
understand their feelings, or talk more openly and
honestly, or feel better about their relationships.

Anna begins by helping Mother.
Mother is learning to set aside some special time to be alone.
She is learning how to ask for privacy when she is working around the
house. Mother is learning to say what she wants calmly and clearly.

And as Mother makes changes in herself,
Christopher discovers that he no longer needs to
fill his ears with cotton balls.

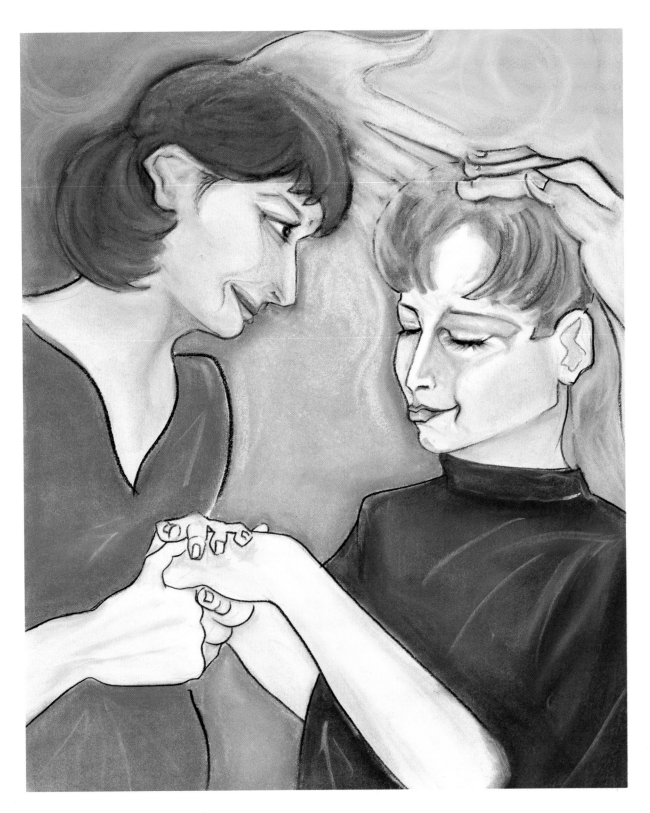

Anna helps Father next.
Father is learning to ask for what he wants without hollering
or hitting. Father is beginning to understand that the people he
loves will respect him if he approaches them with respect.

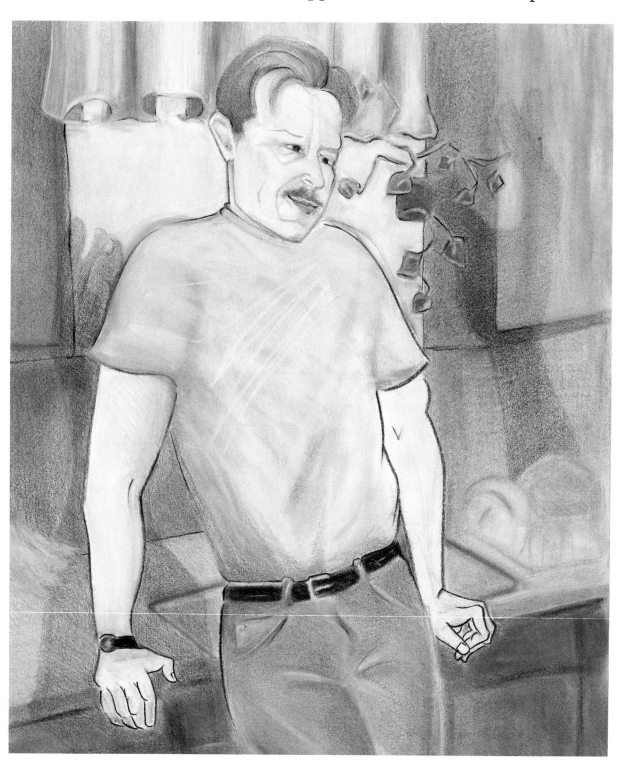

As Father makes changes in himself,
Christopher learns that the stormy sea no longer rises in his stomach.

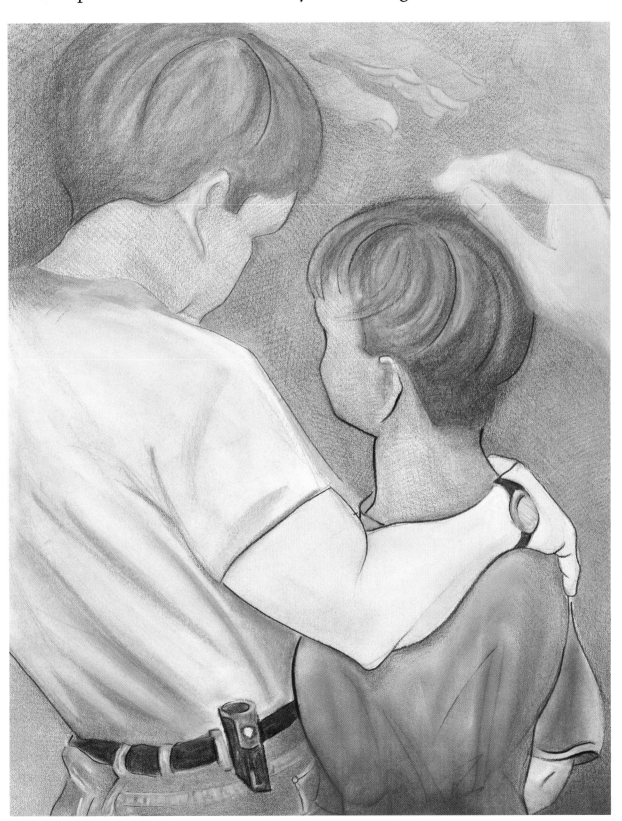

Anna is helping Sister learn that she sets an important example for her brother. She is helping Sister understand that words can be used to express feelings in a loving way.

As Sister makes changes in herself, Christopher finds that
he no longer needs to snake a scarf around his neck.

Anna is helping the family learn to pay attention to
Baby Brother when he cries and makes scary sounds.
As the family responds in healthy ways to Baby Brother,
Christopher no longer needs to coat himself in plastic.

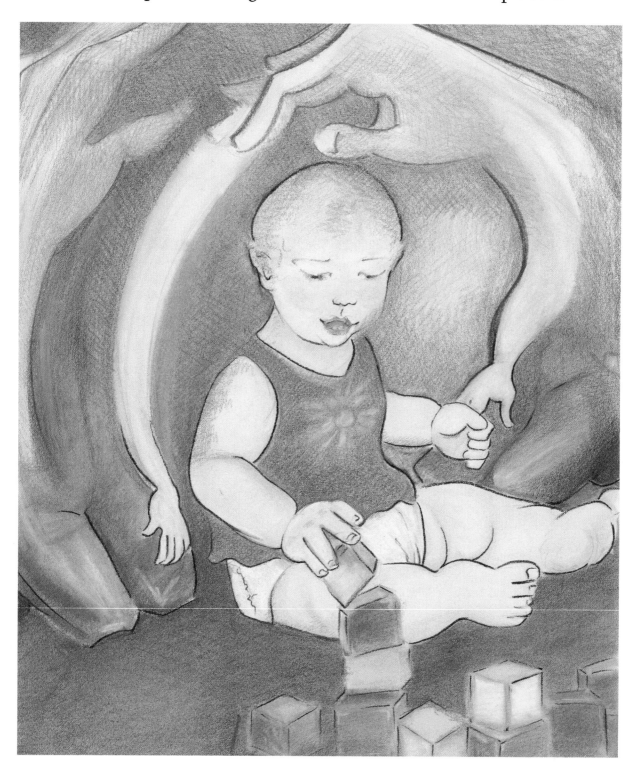

Christopher is also learning that when a black cloud appears over his head, he can break up the darkness with a single thought. He can imagine the sun cutting through the gloom and warming his face. Christopher is learning to use words to express what he needs and wants.

Christopher and his family look forward to seeing Anna.
She is helping them help themselves.

Discussion Questions

What color is your anger?

What does your anger feel like inside your body?

What do you see when you are angry?

What do you hear when you are angry?

When you are angry, do you hurt yourself?

What does your angry behavior look like?

Would you like to be able to express your anger without hurting yourself?

Can you think of five ways to express anger without hurting yourself?

Which of these options is the best way to express your anger?

Do you need help in learning to express your anger in this new way?

What does that help look like?

Who would you ask?

How many times do you think you will have to practice this new way to express your anger before you are successful?

When do you want to start?